THE LITTLE BOOK OF
QUEEN BEY

The wit and wisdom
of Beyoncé

THE LITTLE BOOK OF
QUEEN BEY

The wit and wisdom
of Beyoncé

First published in Great Britain in 2019 by Trapeze
an imprint of The Orion Publishing Group Ltd
Carmelite House, 50 Victoria Embankment
London EC4Y 0DZ

An Hachette UK Company

1 3 5 7 9 10 8 6 4 2

A CIP catalogue record for this book is
available from the British Library.

ISBN (Hardback) 978 1 4091 9164 3
ISBN (eBook) 978 1 4091 9165 0

Printed in Italy

www.orionbooks.co.uk

CONTENTS

BODY POSITIVITY

'IT'S A SILLY SONG, BUT IT'S NICE BECAUSE IT'S MADE CURVY WOMEN FEEL SEXY.'

ON BOOTYLICIOUS, *COSMOPOLITAN*

1 November 2006

'IT'S REALLY ABOUT WHO YOU ARE,
AND THE HUMAN BEING, THAT
MAKES YOU BEAUTIFUL.'

PEOPLE
7 May 2012

'I THINK IT'S IMPORTANT
AND MEN TO
APPRECIATE THE
IN THEIR

FOR WOMEN
SEE AND
BEAUTY
NATURAL BODIES.'

VOGUE
6 August 2018

'IT GETS EASIER TO BE CONFIDENT ABOUT MY BODY AS I GET OLDER.'

COSMOPOLITAN

1 November 2006

'I HAD ALL THE ICE CREAM I WANTED
AND IT WAS THE HAPPIEST TIME
OF MY LIFE.'

THIS MORNING
11 November 2008

'I DON'T KNOW WHAT IT
BUT MY DEFINITION IS

BOUNTIFUL,

SAYS IN THE DICTIONARY, BEAUTIFUL, AND BOUNCIFUL.'

ON BOOTYLICIOUS BEING INCLUDED IN THE DICTIONARY,
LATE SHOW WITH DAVID LETTERMAN
7 February 2006

'MY BIGGEST THING IS TO TEACH [BLUE] NOT TO FOCUS ON THE AESTHETIC.'

PEOPLE

7 May 2012

'YOU CAN'T LET ANYONE TELL YOU
WHAT YOUR BEST IS; YOU KNOW
WHAT YOUR BEST IS.'

CNN
27 June 2011

'TO HAVE THE FREEDOM TO
AND NOT CARE ABOUT
OR FITTING INTO A
REALLY LIBERATING

LET GO OF ALL EGO, WHAT I LOOK LIKE, POPSTAR BOX, WAS TO ME.'

CNN
27 June 2011

'I WANTED EVERYONE
THEIR CURVES,
HONESTY – THANKFUL FOR

TO FEEL THANKFUL FOR THEIR SASS, THEIR THEIR FREEDOM.'

ON HER COACHELLA PERFORMANCE, *HOMECOMING*
17 April 2019

EMPOWERMENT
AND
EQUALITY

'YOUR SELF-WORTH IS DETERMINED BY YOU.'

GQ MAGAZINE
10 January 2013

'DO WHAT YOU WERE BORN TO DO. YOU HAVE TO TRUST YOURSELF.'

COSMOPOLITAN

1 November 2006

'ULTIMATELY YOUR INDEPENDENCE

KNOWING WHO YOU ARE

HAPPY WITH

COMES FROM YOU AND YOU BEING YOURSELF.'

LIFE IS BUT A DREAM
16 February 2013

'IT IS SO LIBERATING TO REALLY KNOW WHAT I WANT, WHAT TRULY MAKES ME HAPPY, WHAT I WILL NOT TOLERATE.'

HARPER'S BAZAAR
11 October 2011

'HUMANITY REQUIRES BOTH MEN AND
WOMEN AND WE ARE EQUALLY IMPORTANT
AND NEED ONE ANOTHER.'

THE SHRIVER REPORT
1 December 2014

'I DON'T LIKE TO GAMBLE, ONE THING I'M WILLING

BUT IF THERE'S TO BET ON, IT'S MYSELF.'

ABC NEWS
24 November 2009

'I'M VERY HAPPY IF

INSPIRE OR

SOMEONE WHO

AN OPPRESSED

MY WORDS CAN EVER

EMPOWER

CONSIDERS THEMSELVES

MINORITY.'

OUT MAGAZINE

8 April 2014

'I'M LEARNING THAT YOU CAN BE KIND AND BE STRONG BUT . . . I HAVE TO BE FAIR TO MYSELF.'

THE OPRAH WINFREY SHOW

11 November 2005

'IT'S IMPORTANT TO MAKE SURE YOU HAVE YOUR OWN LIFE BEFORE YOU'RE SOMEONE ELSE'S WIFE.'

THE OPRAH WINFREY SHOW

13 November 2008

'I FEEL LIKE WHENEVER SOMEONE
AND KINDA TAKES YOU OUT
USUALLY YOU'RE BETTER OFF

MAKES YOU FEEL INSECURE OF WHO YOU REALLY ARE, NOT AROUND THAT PERSON.'

MUCH

14 September 2006

'LESS THAN 100 YEARS AGO, WOMEN DID NOT HAVE THE RIGHT TO VOTE; LOOK HOW FAR WE'VE COME FROM HAVING NO VOICE.'

SPEAKING AT A HILLARY CLINTON RALLY, *CNN*

5 November 2016

'LGBTQI RIGHTS ARE HUMAN RIGHTS.'

GLAAD MEDIA AWARDS
28 March 2019

'IT WAS IMPORTANT TO
HAD NEVER SEEN THEMSELVES
LIKE THEY WERE

ME THAT EVERYONE WHO
REPRESENTED FELT
ON THAT STAGE WITH US.'

ON HER COACHELLA PERFORMANCE, *HOMECOMING*
17 April 2019

MUSIC

'I'VE ONLY SHARED WHO I AM THROUGH MY MUSIC AND I FEEL LIKE THAT MYSTIQUE IS VERY IMPORTANT.'

THE OPRAH WINFREY SHOW
11 November 2005

♬

'ONE OF THE REASONS I CONNECT TO THE SUPER BOWL IS THAT I APPROACH MY SHOWS LIKE AN ATHLETE.'

GQ MAGAZINE
10 January 2013

♫

'SOMETIMES I NEED
WE ALL NEED TO
EMPOWERING
TO

TO HEAR IT MYSELF. HEAR THOSE SONGS REMIND US.'

ON FINDING OUR STRENGTH IN MUSIC, *MARIE CLAIRE*
6 May 2009

'I'M ATTRACTED TO SONGS THAT WILL BECOME A DINNER CONVERSATION!'

BILLBOARD

5 November 2011

♫

'IN MY VIDEOS, I ALWAYS WANT TO BE A POWERFUL WOMAN. THAT'S MY MISSION.'

W MAGAZINE

1 July 2011

♫

49

'THERE'S MY PERSONAL LIFE, AND THEN ME AS SEXY AND

MY SENSITIVE SIDE, A PERFORMER, ENERGIZED AND FUN.'

THE NEW YORK TIMES
14 November 2008

'I ACTUALLY WENT AND BOUGHT TWENTY COPIES OF MY OWN RECORD.'

ON THE LAST THING SHE BOUGHT, *THE TYRA BANKS SHOW*

26 November 2008

♫

'SHE LOOKS UP TO PRINCE.'

ON SASHA FIERCE, *AOL SESSIONS*
13 October 2008

♫

'I WANTED TO SELL
AND I SOLD A
I WANTED TO
I WENT

A MILLION RECORDS, MILLION RECORDS. GO PLATINUM; PLATINUM.'

ELLE
4 December 2008

'I KNOW I'M VERY PRIVATE, BUT I ALWAYS REVEAL MYSELF ON THE STAGE AND I ALWAYS REVEAL MYSELF IN MY MUSIC.'

AOL SESSIONS

13 October 2008

♫

'IT'S FUN AND IT GIVES ME AN EXCUSE TO BLAME ANYTHING BAD ON SASHA FIERCE.'

THE ELLEN DEGENERES SHOW
25 November 2008

CAREER

'I'VE BEEN WORKING NONSTOP SINCE I WAS 15. I DON'T EVEN KNOW HOW TO CHILL OUT.'

ELLE
4 December 2008

'I EMBRACE MISTAKES, THEY MAKE YOU WHO YOU ARE.'

YEAR OF FOUR

30 June 2011

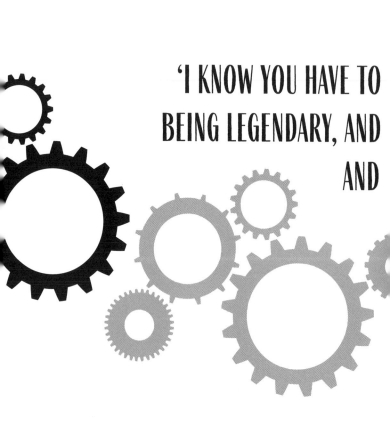

'I KNOW YOU HAVE TO
BEING LEGENDARY, AND
AND

MAKE A TRANSITION INTO

I KNEW THAT IT WAS TIME.

I'M READY.'

THE NEW YORK TIMES
14 November 2008

'I LOVE MY JOB SO THE LEAST I CAN DO IS GIVE MY ALL.'

THE ELLEN DEGENERES SHOW
25 November 2008

'I HAD TO SACRIFICE A LOT GROWING UP . . . AND I DIDN'T GET TO DO A LOT OF THINGS THAT MOST TEENAGE GIRLS DID.'

THE OPRAH WINFREY SHOW
13 November 2008

'THEY WANNA SAY IT'S BECAUSE

IT'S BECAUSE

OF THE SEXY CLOTHES . . . NO! I'M TALENTED.'

NBC NEWS

8 July 2003

'THE OCEAN MAKES ME FEEL REALLY SMALL AND IT PUTS MY WHOLE LIFE INTO PERSPECTIVE.'

YEAR OF FOUR

30 June 2011

'I FEEL LIKE MY JOB IN THE INDUSTRY IS TO PUSH THE LIMITS.'

BILLBOARD

5 November 2011

'I HOPE I CAN CREATE ART

ART THAT **MAKES**

OF

THAT **HELPS PEOPLE HEAL.**
PEOPLE FEEL PROUD
THEIR STRUGGLE.'

ELLE
4 April 2016

'IF EVERYTHING WAS PERFECT YOU WOULD NEVER LEARN AND YOU WOULD NEVER GROW.'

INTERVIEW

2 August 2001

'I WANTED TO FOLLOW IN THE FOOTSTEPS OF MADONNA AND BE A POWERHOUSE.'

CELEBRITY UNIVERSE

21 July 2014

FAMILY
AND
FRIENDS

'WE ARE BEST FRIENDS, WE GREW UP TOGETHER.'

ON DESTINY'S CHILD, *LATE SHOW WITH DAVID LETTERMAN*

7 February 2006

♡

'WE'VE BEEN TOGETHER SINCE I WAS NINE YEARS OLD SO IT'S A FAMILY.'

ON DESTINY'S CHILD, *THE GRAHAM NORTON SHOW*
3 July 2003

'WE'VE LEARNED ABOUT LOYALTY,
AND CARING ABOUT THE PEOPLE
TOGETHER, **HOW TO BE**
WHEN YOU'RE WRONG,

ABOUT THE IMPORTANCE OF LOVING IN THE GROUP, STICKING A FRIEND, HOW TO APOLOGIZE AND HOW TO COMPROMISE.'

ON DESTINY'S CHILD, *INTERVIEW MAGAZINE*
29 January 2013

'I LOVE MY HUSBAND, BUT THERE'S NOTHING LIKE A CONVERSATION WITH A WOMAN WHO UNDERSTANDS YOU.'

LIFE IS BUT A DREAM
16 February 2013

♡

'THE MAIN THING I'VE LEARNED IS NOT TO JUDGE PEOPLE.'

INTERVIEW MAGAZINE

29 January 2013

'SOME OF THE THINGS
DAUGHTERS – ALLOWING
EMOTIONS, THEIR PAIN AND
TO ALLOW AND SUPPORT
BOYS TO DO

THAT WE TEACH OUR THEM TO EXPRESS THEIR VULNERABILITY – WE NEED OUR MEN AND AS WELL.'

ELLE

4 April 2016

'WE'VE SHARED OUR BEST MEMORIES . . .
AND SOME OF OUR HARDEST MOMENTS.'

ON DESTINY'S CHILD, *THE OPRAH WINFREY SHOW*
15 November 2004

'IT'S BEAUTIFUL TO SUPPORT EACH
OTHER AND TO BE SECURE AND BE
HAPPY FOR EACH OTHER.'

THE OPRAH WINFREY SHOW

15 November 2004

'IT'S GREAT TO KNOW THAT

AND THE HEELS AND I'M AT

I HAVE **WARMTH,**

WHEN I TAKE OFF ALL THE MAKEUP
HOME - I HAVE A LIFE, AND
AND I HAVE REALITY.'

TODAY
9 February 2010

'MY MOTHER AND I ARE SO CLOSE AND I ALWAYS PRAYED THAT I WOULD HAVE THAT TYPE OF RELATIONSHIP WITH MY DAUGHTER.'

THE OPRAH WINFREY SHOW
16 February 2013

'I'M JUST SO PROUD OF MY MOM . . .
SHE LED ME BY EXAMPLE.'

ET CANADA

22 September 2011

♡

'SELLING A LOT OF RECORDS,
TO ME, IS NOT SUCCESS; HAPPINESS
IN MY PERSONAL LIFE IS SUCCESS TO ME.'

TODAY TONIGHT

31 July 2009

♡

'AS THE MOTHER OF TWO

ME THAT **THEY**

TOO – IN BOOKS,

GIRLS, IT'S IMPORTANT TO SEE THEMSELVES

FILMS, AND ON RUNWAYS.'

'I WANT MY DAUGHTER TO GROW UP
SEEING A WOMAN LEAD OUR COUNTRY
AND KNOW THAT OUR POSSIBILITIES
ARE LIMITLESS.'

SPEAKING AT A HILLARY CLINTON RALLY, *CNN*

5 November 2016

'WE HAVE TO TEACH OUR GIRLS THAT THEY CAN REACH AS HIGH AS HUMANLY POSSIBLE.'

THE SHRIVER REPORT

1 December 2014

♡